Happier Tomorrow
Happier Today
Happier Right Now

"Short, succinct, powerful. Read it. Apply it. Become happier!"

—Tal ben-Shahar PhD, author of **Happier**

"I can say with certainty that 100% of my clients contact me at least in part because they desire more happiness. **Happier Tomorrow/Today/Right Now** is a gentle, succinct, compulsively readable and practical companion on our shared human search for meaning and fulfillment. One to read again and again!"

—Shannon Kelly, LICSW, PCC, CPCC
Coach, Therapist, Facilitator

"The keys to happiness are eloquently brought out through description, story and the research that proves each key works. It is a reminder that happiness isn't something we have to wait for. It isn't luck. It isn't circumstance or something we are born with. Doors to happiness are everywhere. This book shows us the keys—and all of them work."

—Beulah Trey, PhD. President,
Vector Group Consulting

"No matter where you are—from the sunniest optimist to dreariest pessimist—this book is jam packed with practical wisdom to grow happiness."

—Megan McDonough, CEO, **Wholebeing Institute**

"Usable and accessible—with just the right mix of practical steps and the science that backs them up. I found myself turning pages quickly and thinking about how easy it would be to incorporate these rituals and activities in my own life!"

—Scott Simon, co-founder, **Thrive Cleveland**

"This is a smart, practical, and really enjoyable book. Cohen has a wonderful writing style, and is able to relate important research directly to our everyday lives, showing how we can build happier, more meaningful lives. I'm confident that you'll get a lot out of this book whether you're new to Positive Psychology or have been following it for years."

—Lynda Wallace, Positive Psychology Coach, author of **A Short Course in Happiness**

"This book is not a magic-pill guide to permanent happiness but a smorgasbord of ideas—supported by science, case histories and research—in the pursuit of increased well-being. It is both pragmatic and wise, easy to read and digest. If one book is going to kick-start your journey to a happier life, this is it."

—Fiona Trembath, MAPP, founder, **From Strength to Strength**/Australia

Happier Tomorrow
Happier Today
Happier Right Now

24 *Proven Keys to a More Satisfying Life*

Stuart Cohen

© 2016 by Stuart Cohen. All rights reserved. No part of this book may be reproduced or utilized in any form, or by any electronic, mechanical, or other means, without the prior written permission of the author.

ISBN-10 Number: 0-9833077-3-3
ISBN-13/EAN 13 Number: ISBN-13:978-0-9833077-3-0

Cover Design and Interior Layout: AuthorSupport.com

All rights reserved. No part of this publication may be reproduced, stored in or introduced into a retrieval system, or transmitted in any form or by any means (electronic, mechanical, by photocopying, recording or otherwise) without the prior written permission of the author.

The scanning, uploading, and distribution of this book via the Internet or by any other means without the permission of the author is illegal and punishable by law. Please purchase only authorized printed or electronic editions and do not participate in or encourage electronic piracy of copyrighted materials. The author appreciates your support of author's rights.

*To my daughters Elizabeth and Caroline
who have brought me more happiness
than anything I have ever done.*

Table of Contents

Preface xiii

Introduction xv

1 *It's about Happier* 1

2 *Taking Action* 6

3 *Vision and Goals* 10

4 *Pitfalls along the Way* 13

5 *Resources* 19

6 *12 Keys for Right Now* 27

    Smile Often 27
    Talk with Someone You Care About 30
    Accept Today, Accept Yourself 32
    Perform a Deliberate Act of Kindness 34
    Get Out in Nature 37
    Treat Someone with Compassion 40
    Enjoy/Make Music 43
    Hug Someone 45
    Be Generous 47
    Write about your Feelings 51

    Go for a Walk 53
    Enjoy the Present 55

7 *12 More for a Better Tomorrow* 59

    Lighten Up. 60
    Socialize with Friends More. 62
    Cultivate the Spiritual 64
    Engage in Work that is Meaningful. 66
    Participate in Rituals. 69
    Set Goals and Strive to Achieve Them 72
    Spend on Activities and People, not Things . . 74
    Exercise both the Physical and the Mental. . . 77
    Be Curious 80
    Appreciate and Be Grateful. 81
    Serve Others 84
    Do What you Love 86

8 *Fear and Courage* 90

9 *If You Can Only Do Three* 94

10 *Being True to Yourself* 98

Notes 101

Bibliography. 107

"Happiness is so important it transcends all other worldly considerations"

—**Aristotle**

"The desire for happiness is essential to humans and is the motive for all our actions. The most venerable, clearly understood, enlightened and reliable constant in the word is not only that we want to be happy, but that we want only to be so."

—**St. Augustine,** *The Happy Life*

"Happiness is, for most men, the secret motive of all they do."

—**William James**

"Feelings don't just matter—they are what mattering *means*."

—**Daniel Gilbert**

Preface

I just didn't want to feel so miserable. My desire for a better life led me to major in psychology when I was an undergraduate at Yale years ago. I thought the study of human motivation and behavior would offer a young man like me guidance on how to feel better about myself and my life.

Unfortunately it did not. The field of psychology at the time was oriented entirely to abnormality, dysfunction and mental illness. I couldn't find a single class about how to use the insights of psychology to benefit everyday living. Frustrated, I left the field and became a photographer, but I never lost interest.

After college life became tougher. Following a family crisis and the struggle to find my way, I entered a deep depression that lasted six years. It was difficult to do even simple activities. I had few friends. But even during those years of painful isolation, I knew something better was possible, if only I could break out of the darkness. I felt certain it was possible to have a happy relationship with life.

In time, that happened. I recovered from depression and learned how to live in the world. Eventually I got married, had children and found a photographic specialty that intrigued and engaged me. Life was good. My psychology training never led to a career but it helped with human interaction in many ways, and I never stopped being fascinated with how people think, feel and behave.

With the arrival of the new field of positive psychology, the scientific study of optimal human functioning, in the late 1990's, academic psychology finally began to address the issue of personal well-being. It is exactly what I had been looking for back in college. Here, in concise language, is what I've learned that you can use.

Introduction

Who would like to be happier? Everybody.
Everything you do, in one way or another, you do to become happier. The drive to be happier, in some fashion sooner or later, is the central motivator of human behavior. Even if actions are difficult and involve self-sacrifice, you decide what to do today to become more satisfied, content and happier directly or indirectly eventually.

Happiness, that French scientist turned Buddhist monk Matthieu Ricard defines as "The subjective appreciation of one's own quality of life,"[1] includes both the enjoyment of current pleasure and life-long emotional well-being. The mission of this book is to provide you with simple keys that can move you toward achieving both. The happiness keys here—they are divided into twelve for right now, when you need a lift, and twelve more for the long term—will, if you use them, move you bit by bit upward on the scale of life satisfaction and well-being. The techniques work. Please use them!

You can think of this book as a get-rich scheme for your emotional life. As with getting rich in money, most get-rich *quick* plans are risky and usually fail. Get rich *slowly* methods are more likely to succeed if you stick with them.

The 24 keys cover a wide variety of actions you can do. Some are easy, some take more effort. They may not all suit you equally well. Use the ones that do. Be sure to profit from the short term ones in the moment: they will help lift your mood and get through difficult moments. The longer-term ones will help you build greater life-long satisfaction.

Every one of these keys has been shown to be valid through scientific research by psychologists, researchers and others, presented with each key as "evidence". Only you can make them work in *your* life. I encourage you to go for it.

1

It's About Happier

The pursuit of happiness is really the pursuit of becoming happi*er* as opposed to ever becoming totally happy. It's about the ongoing climb, not some imagined mountaintop.

If you were to chase the end result of being happy you would be pursuing an emotional destination as if, once you arrived there, you could stay that way. That won't happen. There is no such thing as permanent happiness because emotions are fluid: they change constantly.

Even asking the question, "Am I happy?" is not very useful in building a life because it doesn't lead beyond the present moment. It's much better to ask, "How can I become happier?" This question opens up a long view into the future. The answers are likely to lead you to choices and actions that can make your life better, happier and more fulfilling over time.

Not just Pleasure

A happier life is filled with pleasure, but short-term enjoyment is only part of the picture. A pleasurable feeling fades quickly after its moment has passed. The genuinely happier life includes deep contentment and an ongoing sense of well-being.

You should certainly seek out and enjoy pleasurable times, but don't chase them to the exclusion of deeper satisfaction. Becoming happier is a building process that encompasses your whole life. Better to focus on the longest time frame you can imagine.

A Problem with Feelings

Feelings are a powerful indicator of how we're doing, but they change all the time and can be maddeningly unpredictable. Whatever thing, achievement or situation you may think will make you really, really happy won't, at least not for very long. We adapt quickly to both the good—what psychologists call hedonic adaptation—and the bad so that what generated a strong positive or negative feeling once becomes less emotionally charged in relatively short order.

Harvard psychology professor Daniel Gilbert called his terrific book *Stumbling on Happiness* because he found that despite our efforts, we can't really manage our feelings going forward. We are hardwired to expect to feel tomorrow pretty much the same as we feel today, though once tomorrow gets here we may feel differently. That makes it almost impossible to organize our lives around a desired emotion. But the pursuit of happier is much easier.

How It's Done

For the first time in history, there is science behind the desire to be happier. The still-new field of positive psychology has shown us through research that there are certain actions individuals can take that are more likely to lead to us becoming happier over time. We have the understanding. Now all you have to do is follow the steps.

Each person is unique, of course, and the specifics of what one person enjoys might not be exactly the same as what works for someone else. But as Professor Gilbert has pointed out, when it comes to our emotional functioning we all operate in pretty much the same way. That's why you can trust the 24 keys presented here to be valid for you too. Not all of them will be equally useful. But if you follow this guidance and stick with it, you will likely enjoy a happier life.

What is Possible

Happier is possible for everyone. But an upbeat, happy personality day in and day out might not be. Psychologist Jonathan Haidt says, "Each person has a characteristic level of happiness...not so much a set point but a potential range,"[2] Happier means spending more time at a higher point within your range.

Recent discoveries have shown how large a part genes play in determining basic temperament, the overall tendency to be cheerful, melancholy, tranquil, etc. Genes account for about 60% of our disposition. That's good to know if you are thinking your normal temperament should be like someone else's. It shouldn't. Your emotional state is unique to you and should never be compared to the subjective experience of someone else. You still have 40% you can influence with your thoughts and actions, a large enough percentage that it is definitely worth making the effort.

Unselfishness of Happiness

Many people cannot avoid the voices of their childhood that told them that pursuing their own happiness was selfish and therefore bad. That's simply wrong. Happier people are actually *less* selfish than others. They are more relaxed and open than unhappy people and are likely to be more generous. Matthieu Ricard, who has been called "the happiest man in the world," writes in his book *Happiness*, "Those who believe themselves to he happiest are also the most altruistic."[3] Movement toward becoming happier affects other people and can influence them in a positive direction too. Becoming happier is good not just for you but also for those around you.

Positive emotion is contagious like smiles and laughter. Growing happier is one of the most unselfish things you can do because it leads to sharing the good feeling. The flame of a candle can light hundreds or thousands of other candles without itself being diminished. Becoming happier works the same way. Everybody wins.

2

Taking Action

"...a real increase in your own happiness is in fact attainable, if you are prepared to do the work. If you make a decision to be happier in your life, and you understand that this is a weighty decision that will take effort, commitment, and a certain amount of discipline, know that you can make it happen."[4]

If you truly want a happier life, action makes all the difference. No amount of hoping, wishing, thinking and planning compares to acting on your own behalf. To change the way it has been to the way you want it to be, you have to act.

Action gets you going. It builds momentum toward your goals. Once you start to act in line with the keys recommended here, your satisfaction is bound to grow. On the other hand, if you are hoping to find magic in these pages that will turn your life around simply by reading, knowing, or believing, you are likely to be disappointed.

Twenty-five centuries ago Aristotle, the Greek philosopher, emphasized that character arises from activities. What we do makes us who we are. Whatever your background, wherever you have succeeded or failed in the past, you can start today to make your life better and more the way you want it to be.

Patient Progress

Take small steps. Pick a few of the happiness keys and begin today. Try them on like a piece of clothing and wear them around for a while. See if they fit. Find the ones that suit you, at least at first, and let them guide you. Be sure to acknowledge your successes, even minor ones. Imagine yourself as an athlete getting into shape after a long layoff. It doesn't always feel comfortable even when you know what you are doing is right. Focus on a vision of your life as you'd like to imagine it and press forward.

This may sound simple but it is not easy. You are retraining yourself from old ways to new ones. That is why it is so important to take action on your own behalf, even in small steps, over time.

Focus on the Long Term

The demands of the moment often require you to act on what needs attention right now. But action in service of your longer-term aspirations will ultimately lead to greater satisfaction. It's the difference between getting caught up in what feels urgent versus focusing on what is truly important.[5]

Take a moment to imagine what will be important months or years from now. Can you picture that far ahead? If you can't, let your mind wander farther into the future than you normally do. Develop a mental picture of how you'd like your life to be in a year, or five, or ten years. Don't let short-term thinking distract you. A long-term perspective is better to guide your actions in service of what matters most.

Find a Buddy or Cheerleader

Change is easier when you don't have to do it alone. The support of a buddy, even one friend or family member, increases the odds of your success. Research confirms this.

A widely cited study concludes, "...social support is ... an asset in enabling a person to persist at a task under frustrating conditions."[6]

Don't hide what you are doing. It's common to not tell anyone when trying to accomplish something ambitious so that you won't look bad should you fail. The commitment to succeed will get stronger if you announce your determination to at least one person. On the other hand, don't talk about it so much to so many people that your words overwhelm your actions. You must act.

Find a cheerleader who believes in you. Better still, recruit a partner and walk this path together. Encouraging someone else to take steps toward a happier life will reinforce your own efforts. Besides, it's more fun if you do it together.

Making a better life is not a casual decision. Think if this is something you truly want and if now is the right time. If it is, make an action plan: your actions will make all the difference.

3

Vision and Goals

A vision orients everything you do around where you want to end up. Goals provide the visible markers of your progress.

Start with a Vision

A vision is simply a picture of what the end result you want looks like. It grows out of your imagination. Take a few minutes to imagine yourself as you want to be, and imagine the life you want to be living. Make the picture rich with detail. Write the vision down as a story with as many specifics as you can. Adjust when necessary and read it often. Once a day is ideal, especially on days you don't feel like it.

Set Specific Goals

The more specific your goals are, the more clearly you can focus on them. Goals should be clear enough that you will know when you've achieved them and challenging enough so that you care. Current goal theory tells us that more demanding goals elicit higher levels of performance as long as the person is reasonably confident of being able to succeed.[7]

If where you live is not satisfactory, make a goal of living in the home that's right for you. If you have a long-term project in the works, make a goal of seeing it completed successfully. Good health is a worthwhile goal for anybody.

Even the goal of being happier is too general to act on. What are the specifics? What will it look like once you have gotten there?

Spend what time it takes to write down goals including what happier would look like for you. Make a list of 3 – 10 items written in the present tense as already accomplished, and put it up where you can see it. Be sure to choose goals you can picture as already done and ones you will recognize once they have been reached.

Examples of good "happier" goals:

- I am more at peace with myself than ever
- I go to bed at night satisfied with my day.
- The work I do is satisfying and meaningful.

- I have wonderful friends.
- I have a healthy diet.

Examples of less effective goals:

- I smile a lot.
- My dreams are coming true.
- I don't beat myself up anymore.
- Everybody I meet likes me.
- I eat only healthy food always.

Reminding yourself of your goals drives home the message that they matter. Emotionally rich mental pictures of your goals already realized are powerful: picturing what it will look like when they have been achieved increases the likelihood of that happening. When you achieve one, congratulate yourself, cross it off the list, tell someone and replace it with another.

Work goals need deadlines but goals on the way to becoming happier do not. That's because there is no final end to greater well-being. There can always be more. Stick with your goals and keep at it, even as you encounter disappointment. Perseverance indicates to your inner self that you genuinely care. Never, never, never give up.

4

Pitfalls along the Way

Any time you try to make big changes, the patterns of your previous behavior automatically try to assert themselves. You may start to *feel* as though the change you seek is too difficult or not worth the effort. This is due to *homeostasis*, the tendency of all kinds of systems to resist change, and it is normal. Homeostasis is a force that tries to keep everything as it has been. It slows down attempts at change and makes you wonder if what you are trying to do is worthwhile.

Notice when this happens, but don't give in to it. Overcome homeostasis by taking regular action even when you don't feel like it. Through action you send a strong message to your inner self that what you want *now* is more important than the way it used to be.

Among the pitfalls you are likely to bump up against are four illusions that might sound helpful but are not.

In the pursuit of happiness these are the allure of change for its own sake, the necessity of self-discipline, the problem-solving approach and the urgency of now.

Allure of Change for its own Sake

The idea of change for its own sake is a powerful motivator to try something new. When we say, "I need a change," what we're expressing is a desire to get away from the current situation. You might assume without much thought, when you're unhappy, that change will automatically be for the best. But often it doesn't work out that way.

Chances are, much of your life is already the way you want it. After all, you set it up that way either deliberately or by default in the course of making everyday decisions. Unless you're in a really awful place, beware of yearning for change without having a direction in mind. Change just for the sake of change may end up generating as much bad as good.

There is a better way to think about changing life for the better, and that is in terms of creating.* Whether or

---

* An expert on creating, in the ordinary sense of generating something new, is Robert Fritz. His books *The Path of Least Resistance* and *Creating* are wonderful guides to making up your life as you want it. He teaches classes, too. Check out his website, www.robertfrtiz.com.

not you are a "creative" person in the sense of the arts, you naturally create all the time when you make things up. You make up what to have for lunch or where to go on vacation. You make up how you want your hair to look and your style of dress. This is creating at the most basic level, something you do every day.

Creating a happier life is not simply change in the sense of getting away from a less happy one. Becoming happier moves you toward a desired future, not just away from an unwanted past. Focus on that desired future and take steps to get there. The right amount of change will happen.

Self-discipline

Do you lack the self-discipline to make major changes? So does most everyone else. I don't know anyone who claims to have a lot of it. I certainly don't.

Self-discipline is not the point when it comes to building a happier life: wanting that life is. If you want it and are able to tolerate the doubts and setbacks associated with homeostasis, self-discipline doesn't enter into the picture.

The best response to address the self-discipline illusion is a clear vision. Imagine what happier would look like for you. Rather than imagine everything blissfully perfect, create a picture of being a little happier. If you rate your current happiness on a scale of 1 – 10, what would it look like to be one notch happier? Moving up the scale a little is much easier to imagine. Focus on that. When becoming just a bit happier is within your reach, self-discipline stops mattering.

Problem-solving

Creating a happier life is not an exercise in problem solving. You won't become happier by trying to solve the problem of being unhappy. It doesn't work that way.

The reason is because problem-solving is about fixing what's broken, getting rid of something bad instead of creating something good. Problem-solving is about relief from difficulty. That's not the same as having more joy in life.

Many people find the problem-solving approach attractive because problems are easy to identify. We all have them. But when you do that, what's bad—the problem—sets the agenda. In creating a happier life, *you* set the agenda. You make choices consistent with the life you want and take steps based on what you *do* want rather than on what you *don't* want any more.

Getting rid of a bad thing does not necessarily bring you a good thing. Put your attention on the good you want to generate. When you succeed, the problems will seem to vanish on their own.

The Urgency of Now

In our era of instant gratification, many people are impatient. We want what we want and we want it right now. But we don't achieve anything meaningful instantaneously. In this moment the best we can do is relieve temporary suffering, and Chapter 6 provides a dozen keys that will help you do just that.

Building a happier full life takes time, though not necessarily all that long. If you start to act and stick with it, you should feel a difference within a month. That's a fair time period to commit to right at the beginning. If you stay with it, there is no upper limit to how much you can improve your sense of well-being. Just don't delude yourself into thinking it will happen overnight or today's good feeling, when you have it, will last forever.

The process of building a happier life is organic. It grows at different speeds and sometimes in unpredictable directions. Learn from what it teaches you. Setbacks are going to occur when you may feel as though you are going backwards. So what? That happens to everyone. Turn your attention back to the vision of the happier life you want and move on.

And don't check in too often to see how you are doing. Frequent self-evaluation won't help and might hurt.

5

Resources

Most of what you need to grow happier is already part of you and me, as it is for everyone. The trick is to find those resources inside and to use them. At the same time, recognize that we have lurking within us voices from the past that could sabotage our best efforts. Which voices to listen to and which ones to ignore makes all the difference.

Key inner resources to take advantage of include attention, enthusiasm, the truth, personal strengths, and memory. The most valuable resource that comes from outside is the support of others.

Attention

Multi-tasking is simply not real for most people. We only put our attention on one thing at a time. How you manage your singular attention—and you *can* manage it—makes some things more important than others. When you focus on what matters most you naturally open yourself to new ideas, new connections and new learning.

Our minds wander easily. When that happens, and it will, practice bringing it back to what you want to be thinking about: your work, creative efforts, people you care about or anything else. It's not hard to do, just drop one thought by replacing it with another. You don't even need a lot of self-discipline. When your mind wanders again, bring it back again.

Other people's interests will try to grab your attention at every turn through advertising, promotional messages and especially the Internet. Some of those messages are well designed to appear "interesting," and some may genuinely appeal to you. But they are all trying to advance someone else's agenda rather than yours. Protect your attention by deciding in advance what you will let distract you and what you won't. In the same way, the best way to avoid telephone calls interrupting your family dinner is to decide before you sit down that you are not going to answer the phone if it rings while you are eating.

Managing attention can be challenging but it's easy to learn if you try. Start by deciding what you are going to think about and keep returning to that when your mind drifts. Build your skill in making best use of your precious attention.

Enthusiasm

Enthusiasm is GREAT! When your enthusiasm is high that feeling of power and confidence makes it easier to take on anything. Use moments of enthusiasm to charge forward toward what your heart desires.

Enthusiasm does not guarantee success, of course. It is a feeling, and like other feelings, it rises and falls unpredictably. You are not going to feel it every minute no matter how authentic the desire, and a drop-off in enthusiasm does not mean anything is wrong. That's why needing to feel enthusiastic before you can take a bold step is a recipe for failure. When you're feeling it, use enthusiasm to push forward. At the same time, make yourself into someone who can act as needed even when that enthusiastic feeling is not there.

The Truth

Whether the truth is pleasant or uncomfortable, it's the only sound basis for moving forward. It's worth making the effort to distinguish what is true from what you'd like to be true or fear might be true.

Sometimes you have to step back from the emotions of the moment to recognize the truth in any situation. Since we all desire a positive future, we may ignore warning signs of trouble and get caught up in too rosy a view. Or we might exaggerate obstacles and end up talking ourselves out of even trying. Better to seek a balanced and honest view even if we have to dig deeper to find out what that is.

When something is complicated and important, drill down on the details and the people involved so as to reveal the truth as best you can. That may include learning more about yourself. Knowing the truth grounds your efforts and saves you from disappointment.

Get to know the people around you as they are, the parts you like and those you don't. That way you'll know who you can count on. And you won't end up feeling betrayed when someone turns out to be less reliable than you had hoped for. Most people are decent and everyone has weaknesses. Learn the truth about who people are so you will know accurately what to expect.

Strengths

Everybody has more talent and skills in some areas compared to others. What are yours? What do *you* naturally do best and enjoy?

Whenever you can, choose activities that engage your strengths, that come easily and you like doing. You will be happier and more successful. Too many people put a disproportionate effort into trying to correct their weaknesses. That may be necessary at times, but not all weak areas need fixing. Many can be ignored or worked around. You'll make more progress and have a better time becoming great at what you're already good at.

Look for ways to use your strengths to make any task more accessible. There is almost always more than one way to proceed, and what seems like the obvious way might not be the best way for you. Think about how your unique strengths can guide your approach to solving problems and reaching goals.

If you are not sure what your strengths are, or even if you think you know, there is an easy way to find out. The VIA Institute on Character will tell you online at www.viacharacter.org. Take the free survey. The 24 strengths listed include kindness, teamwork, love of learning and others. Once you know what your individual strengths are, you can organize your life in favor of activities that call for what you're already good at and steer away from tasks that suit you less well. When difficulties arise, see how you can resolve them through those same strengths instead of battling what you don't want to do anyway. Why beat your head against a wall?

Memory

Use your memory to make you happier. As much as you can, remember the good things and try to forget the bad. A life full of happy memories feels a lot better than carrying around remembrances of disappointment.

Too many people do just the opposite: they remember their mistakes and beat themselves up over them. That's silly. If advising a friend, would you recommend remembering good things that happened or reliving suffering and failure?

There may be valuable lessons from past difficulties. Learn the lessons and let the painful memory fade. There is no benefit in recalling how bad it was. Once you've learned the lesson you don't need hold onto the pain.

We all have selective memory: we remember some things and not others. It can be an ally or a curse. If you're in the habit of remembering the bad and forgetting the good, retrain yourself by making a point to recall something good that happened every time you find yourself feeling badly about some past failure. Nobody said you have to be perfect all the time: you're human after all. Retraining takes a while, but can be done. Start today to make selective memory work for you rather than against you.

Support

The key resource that comes from outside you is the support of friends, family members, coworkers and others. Their impact on almost everything we do is greater than most people realize. Humans are social animals who are heavily influenced by positive and negative reinforcement. That's why you should surround yourself with supportive people. You will increase your chances of success by having friends who genuinely want you to succeed in improving your life. Their support will prove valuable in good times and bad.

Be aware that some people won't like it if you change, even if you change for the better. Those who expect you to be the same as you have always been—because of *their* homeostasis—may feel uncomfortable as your life improves. Over time you may find yourself shifting your group of friends in the direction of positive people who will reinforce the person you are becoming. Who you hang around with matters. Choose cheerful people who support the person you are striving to become.

6

12 Keys for Right Now

These twelve keys are actions you can do now to feel better right away and begin to build toward a happier future. Think of them as a tool kit you can use again and again. Each one is accompanied by a story of how someone benefited from using the key (the case history) and scientific research validation (the evidence). You will find that some of these keys suit you better than others. Do what works.

The effect of these actions is short term. In many cases the benefit won't last once you stop. Doing them repeatedly for years will have an enduring effect.

1 Smile Often

Smiling not only reflects happiness, it inspires it. When your face lights up in a genuine smile, you feel more relaxed and happier. Psychologists use the term "Duchenne" smile to indicate an authentic smile that includes the mouth and the small muscles around the eyes. A forced smile that shows up only on the lips does not have the same effect.

A happy thought may be all it takes to have something to smile about. Recall a pleasurable moment or the picture of someone you love. If imagining a happy image doesn't come easily, try harder to find one. Or simply think of yourself happy for the instant it takes to evoke a smile.

See if you can develop a habit of smiling for no reason at all. Try it right now! Even a fleeting smile lightens your countenance and lifts the weight of a heavy mood. A smile makes you appear more accessible to others, which stimulates interaction and relationship. Even when busy, deliberately putting a smile on your face will benefit you. One smile inspires another, it may help others around you feel better too. Commit to smiling ten or more times a day even when there is no specific reason to do so. You will feel more relaxed and happier.

Case history: When I worked as a photographer, I used to spend weeks in foreign countries hunting for photos of people and events. I enjoyed it, but it required intense focus and could be exhausting. Someone told me that all that intensity put people off and that I should smile more. What a difference that made! When I smiled more, people were more willing to interact with me and the photography improved. An even bigger benefit was that I was less tired at the end of the day, as all those smiles relaxed me physically as well.

Evidence: James D. Laird of Clark University found that subjects who were instructed to smile as part of an experiment reported more positive feelings than those who were asked to frown. Cartoons viewed while subjects were following the instruction to smile were reported as more humorous than cartoons viewed while they were frowning.[8] The act of smiling clearly made a difference.

Even better, smiles are contagious: they make other people feel better too. Research by S. Douglas Pugh of UNC/Charlotte showed that employee smiling in business interactions made customers feel better about a service interaction and report better service quality.[9]

2 Talk with Someone You Care About

Few things lift your mood as readily as sharing a moment's conversation with a close friend or family member. Humans are by nature social, we do better and feel better in relationship with people we care about. Conversation with a good friend rewards you both.

This is especially true when face-to-face, usually true over the telephone and often true when using electronic media. A conversation with someone you like goes deeper than the topic at hand. It reinforces your relationship history that may include many pleasant interactions over a long time. Sharing with a friend brings out the sense of connectedness inherent in all positive emotions. That is true whether you are talking about anything meaningful or just chatting.

Lonely or depressed people who feel they have few friends and nobody to talk to may worry about "imposing" on others by asking them to talk or get together. You always have much in common with others in the shared experience of being human and alive. Find something you share to talk about: the news, sports, even the weather. You and the other person will feel better for the interaction.

Case history: A woman I know would spend an hour or more on the phone every week talking about nothing to her parents back home in another state. For people who knew each other well it seemed an extremely shallow conversation. Nobody said anything of consequence.

It turns out they weren't having a real conversation at all, they were visiting. The content of their words meant little. It was sharing together for that hour that enriched their lives out of the strength of their love for each other.

Evidence: A study by Cendri A. Hutcherson et. al. of Stanford states, "The need for social connection is a fundamental human motive, and it is increasingly clear that feeling socially connected confers mental and physical health benefits."[10]

Daniel Kahneman writes: "It is only a slight exaggeration to say that happiness is the experience of spending time with people you love and who love you."[11]

Ed Diener and Martin Seligman, two of the leaders in the field of positive psychology, conclude: "No variable was sufficient for happiness, but good social relations were necessary."[12]

3 Accept Today, Accept Yourself

Whether you like where you are in the long arc of your life or not, right now here you are. Welcome to today! Whatever path got you here is now behind you, part of your past. Today's current reality is the starting point for whatever comes next, the only solid basis on which to move forward.

Accepting today means coming to some level of peace with where you are now. You don't have to like it or want it to continue the same way for even another minute. Simply acknowledge how it is now. If this doesn't come easily, start by describing your reality as accurately as you can without judgment: "This is what my life looks like today." Resist the temptation to find fault with the parts you don't like.

The second part, often more difficult, is to accept yourself just the way you are. Again, you don't have to like it all. You may want to make changes tomorrow. Whatever aspects of yourself you don't like you came by honestly in the course of growing up and living with other people. You are human and made mistakes just like everybody else. Once you accept that, you've got the firm ground on which to build whatever comes next.

Though many people find it difficult to do, acceptance of self is *the* key step in self love. Do your best to release painful feelings about the past. Just let them go. Forgive yourself and those who harmed you. Drop the guilt that can make it more likely to repeat past errors. You tried your best, sometimes it worked, sometimes it didn't. The past is over. It can't hurt you now unless you let it. Accept who you are and where you are right now, and turn your focus forward.

Case history: I have great respect for people in Recovery such as those in Alcoholics Anonymous and other 12-step programs. Week in and week out, often for decades, their dedication to living healthy, happy lives brings them to meetings that help them stay sober. Those meetings begin and end with the famous Serenity Prayer that begins, "God give me the strength to accept the things I cannot change..." Acceptance is the necessary first action on the way to serenity for them, and maybe for you too.

The idea is much older. Epictetus (55 – 135 CE), a Roman philosopher, said, "There is only one way to happiness and that is to cease worrying about things which are beyond the power of our will."[13] Epictetus taught that suffering arises from trying to control what is uncontrollable, also from neglecting to do that which is in our power. His message has stood the test of time.

Evidence: Professors Ellen Langer and Shelley Carson of Harvard write: "Self-acceptance is crucial to mental health. The absence of ability to unconditionally accept oneself can lead to a variety of emotional difficulties..." Their research showed that people who are evaluating themselves rather than accepting themselves are more likely to be unhappy and unable to function at optimal levels. The article recommends mindfulness as an effective path to self-acceptance.[14]

John Chamberlain and David Haaga, writing about how to achieve a high sense of self worth, suggest that people are happier when they don't bother to evaluate themselves at all: "Any level of self-esteem reflects a dysfunctional habit of globally evaluating one's worth; it would be preferable to accept oneself unconditionally."[15]

4 Perform a Deliberate Act of Kindness

Helping other people makes you feel better right away. Even simple acts of kindness count. While most of us are nice to others often, intentional acts of kindness—doing something deliberately to help someone else—will brighten your mood in the moment and perhaps for much longer.

Acts of kindness can be very simple such as helping a child or elderly person through a moment's difficulty. Better still, planning to treat others with kindness and then doing so lifts your whole day. What might you do tomorrow to show kindness to someone, even someone you do not know?

Acting with kindness lifts your mood in part because it takes your attention off yourself. During low moments, we tend to focus thinking on ourselves and how we are feeling. The shift to being of service to others changes that. You get to feel good about yourself for doing so and may get the added benefit of someone else's warm thanks. Over time, repeatedly performing deliberate kindness raises your self-image as you come to see yourself as a better person.

Case history: The New York Times reported an outbreak of kindness at drive-thru restaurants in the U.S. and Canada. Drivers would get to the pay window to pick up their orders and find that the driver before them had already paid for their food.[16] The gesture was anonymous since the one who paid had already driven off and could not even be thanked.

It's called "paying it forward", performing a kindness for a stranger with no intention to be paid back. A Tim Horton's restaurant in Winnipeg, Manitoba, claimed that 228 consecutive cars paid it forward one day. Other fast food restaurants in Texas, Massachusetts and Michigan have seen dozens in a row do it, though generally it happens in isolated cases.

You can pay it forward in many ways. Put a coin in an expired parking meter to help someone you don't know avoid a ticket. Give even a single flower to a shut-in. Do something meaningful that you can afford. Catherine Hyde Ryan, author of the book *Pay It Forward*, calls it "goodness gone viral." Who wouldn't want to be a part of that?

Evidence: Sonja Lyubomirsky of University of California Riverside instructed subjects in an experiment, *"In our daily lives, we all perform acts of kindness for others... One day each week, you are to perform five acts of kindness. The acts do not need to be for the same person,* *the person may or may not be aware of the act."* The intention to be kind made a difference over and above the actions themselves. Those who committed to performing 5 deliberate acts of kindness one day a week were significantly happier for it, moreso even than those who performed kindnesses on a regular basis. The intention to be kind made that much of a difference.[17]

In a controlled study by Kristin Layous et. al., 9 – 11 year old children in Vancouver instructed to perform acts of kindness to others were compared to children given other tasks. The subjects felt better about themselves and gained greater peer acceptance. "Our study demonstrates that doing good for others benefits the givers, earning them not only improved well-being but also popularity."[18]

5 Get Out in Nature

Simply getting outdoors in Nature can calm your worries and lift your mood. Walking among trees, in the rain, or sitting on a park bench listening to birds can make you feel significantly happier, especially on a difficult day.

Most people intuitively understand that being out in

Nature makes us feel better. Wild natural places present all sorts of new things to notice, but even a manicured city park offers opportunities to get away from your worries. To maximize the benefit, pay close attention to the details of what you see, hear and smell. Look at the shapes and colors of the leaves and flowers. Listen to the different voices of birds or the sound of the wind. Notice the smell of the sea, or flowers, or pine trees.

Discovering the details of Nature is a delight. The closer you pay attention, the more you will notice and the easier it will be to leave your worries behind. Getting outdoors in Nature to walk, run, ski, or play is a proven happiness strategy. Those who do it regularly get that benefit again and again.

Case history: When I lived in a coastal New England town, every day I'd see runners, walkers and those out for a stroll with the dog along the beach. The pleasure of being by the seaside with the endless view, the smell of the ocean and the lapping of the waves brought people back again and again.

Urban parks achieve the same effect for city dwellers. On weekends Central Park in New York City is alive with thousands of New Yorkers taking a break from the intensity of the city among the trees, lakes and meadows of the park.

You have probably done this yourself, gone out into Nature and returned refreshed. When conditions permit, it's one of the easiest ways to enhance your feeling of well-being.

Evidence: The research overwhelmingly supports the beneficial effects of being outside in natural surroundings. Jo Barton and Jules Pretty of the Interdisciplinary Centre for Environment and Society in England performed a meta-analysis of 10 studies involving 1252 participants. They concluded, "Every green environment improved both self-esteem and mood."[19] The researchers also determined that time spent out in Nature is salutary for the mentally ill.

Researchers George MacKerron and Susana Mourato, in a study of 22,000 participants, determined that happiness is greater in natural environments. "When outdoors, every habitat type except inland bare ground is associated with significantly higher happiness levels than the continuous urban type." Coastal environments, by the sea or large lakes, proved especially effective at lifting mood.[20]

Esther Sternberg M.D. reports that hospital patients in rooms with a beautiful view of natural surroundings recover at a significantly faster rate than those whose windows look out on other buildings.[21] Even in an airtight hospital room the view of a natural environment makes a positive difference.

6 Treat Someone with Compassion

Nothing gets your mind off your problems faster than having compassion for someone else. Compassion means feeling strongly for or with another person, usually when that person is having a difficult time. It is reaching out with your feelings to the shared experience of being human.

This is not the same thing as feeling badly for someone in pain, and it is surely unlike feeling sorry for him or her. When you feel badly for someone, the focus is still on yourself and how *you* feel. Feeling sorry for someone emphasizes the separation between you and another: 'It's unfortunate that you're having a hard time but I'm still fine.'

Compassion is different. In compassion we willingly

share the human condition with someone in pain. It starts with empathy, the ability to imagine how another person feels and feel, to some degree, that way too. We imagine how difficult a time that person is having and wish for them to be released from suffering.

Self-compassion—treating oneself with kindness, care, and concern in the face of negative life events—has come to light in recent years as a key behavior in enhancing well-being. Kristin Neff, PhD, in her book *Self Compassion: Stop Beating Yourself up and Leave Insecurity Behind,* describes compassion as involving "feelings of kindness for people who are suffering, so that the desire to help, to ameliorate suffering, emerges." Her book is a plea for readers to treat themselves with the same kindness and care they might devote to others. If you are particularly hard on yourself, exploration of the literature on self-compassion may be helpful to you.

Case history: When one of my daughters was a teenager, she developed a serious illness. She could have died. Thankfully, her recovery is strong and the terror of that time is behind us, hopefully forever. But I remember how desperate and lonely it felt.

Whenever I meet people who are suffering on behalf of their children due to illness, drugs or for any other reason, I do my best to offer compassion. I can't solve their problems. But I remember how much the emotional support of others meant to me during that troubled time. I go out of my way to offer the same kind of caring and compassion. I know what a simple act of heartfelt sharing means to people who may feel terribly alone in their struggle. They truly appreciate whatever words of comfort I might provide. And it's meaningful to me. It makes me feel better to lighten someone else's load, if only for a moment.

The Dalai Lama, spiritual leader of Tibetan Buddhists and a Nobel Peace Prize laureate, says simply, "If you want others to be happy, practice compassion. If you want to be happy, practice compassion."

Evidence: Canadian researcher Myriam Mongrain et. al., using over 700 volunteer subjects, showed that those who acted compassionately toward others reported improvements in happiness and self-esteem compared to those who performed some neutral task. This was especially true for those who suffered from high levels of anxiety. They concluded, "Of notable relevance to mental health, compassion is not only a process that builds positive relationships with others; it is also a vital path to releasing the human mind from the effects of harmful negative emotions."[22]

A step-by-step approach to becoming a more compassionate person can be found at http://www.wikihow.com/Cultivate-Compassion-in-Your-Life

7 Enjoy/Make Music

Music has a powerful influence on emotions. You have probably already used music to influence your mood countless times. Music channels attention away from the concerns of the day into melody and rhythm. Beyond distracting you, it can uplift you. When you want to lift your emotions and feel better, music is an easy way.

If you make music, either play an instrument or sing, you are especially fortunate. Making music is a mindful activity that requires full attention, whether or not you have great musical talent or skill. Even casual musicians love what happens when they begin to play an instrument or sing, especially when they do it with others.

Case history: I use different kinds of music for different occasions. When I used to spend hours in a darkroom printing photographs, I listened to jazz exclusively. It just seemed right. In moments when I feel beaten down and need rest I choose Baroque music, especially Bach. When cooking a big meal I generally end up listening to opera arias, and long drives in the car naturally seem to call for country music.

Your style might be completely different. If you are a musician, you could have much more sophisticated musical tastes. A lawyer I know who has sung in public all his life calls singing "the best soul medicine I know."

Evidence: The notion that music influences feelings is so universally known that most research addresses the particulars, such as how certain types of music affect mood and to what degree. A comparison of data from several studies showed how music affects physiological responses, such as breathing, pulse rate, blood pressure and galvanic skin response.[23] A study of heart attack patients in a hospital showed that those subjected to music therapy, basically listening to relaxing music, had fewer complications and reported lower stress levels than the control group.[24]

Many books are available on Music Therapy, the clinical field that uses music to improve mental and physical health.

8 Hug Someone

Martha Bolton in *The Official Hugs Book* writes, "A hug has the power to heal broken relationships and wounded spirits. It has even been known to heal physical ailments. A hug is reassurance when we're down, hope in hopeless situations, and the best way to communicate affection when words seem inadequate."[25]

A hug is an astonishing gesture. Hugs turn the shared experience of being human into an act of physical intimacy. Hugs are direct human connection at its most explicit.

Unless you feel forced to hug someone against your will, a hug cannot help but make you feel better. Mental chatter disappears as the physical sensation of hugging someone you care about brings you close. It reinforces the feeling of connection that is at the heart of our emotional system.[26]

Case history: John Sexton, former president of New

York University, is known for hugging just about everyone he meets including students. It's part of his managerial style, and he estimates he hugs on average about 50 people a day. Hugging, he believes, breaks down the artificial barrier between two people of different social standing. It is his way to facilitate the communication needed to be an effective leader.

Traditions of hugging vary from culture to culture. In some cultures women greet with a hug and men shake hands. In others male friendship hugging has been normal for a long time. The hug of love is a universal gesture of sharing this life together.

Evidence: A study at Penn State University divided a population into two groups and assigned one group to hug at least five people a day for four weeks. Some subjects, mostly men, found it awkward at first but managed. The hugging group became significantly happier.[27]

Howard Bloom, in his book *The Lucifer Principle*, considers hugging children to be a force in shaping what kind of adults they become. He reports: "The societies that hugged their kids were relatively peaceful. The cultures that treated their children coldly produced brutal adults."[28]

Judith Weisberg and Maxine Haberman report on the effects of physical contact in nursing homes: "Elderly nursing home residents have a heightened need for affectionate touch and are particularly sensitive to its benefits. This inspired two social workers to develop a 'hugging week,' celebrating the theme of affection throughout a geriatric facility. This innovative program had positive effects not only on the residents but on family and staff members as well."[29]

9 Be Generous

Giving makes people happier. However you do it, be generous to the degree you can afford. There are many options:

Donate to charity. Whether you can make a large gift to a museum or give a small amount to a charitable organization whose mission you agree with, giving feels good. It strengthens your connection with your values. It feels profoundly moral. It expands your sense of yourself by aligning you with a cause that is greater than any one person.

Spend money on behalf of someone you care about

instead of yourself. Even a small gift, given with affection, makes you both feel wonderful. Do it because you want to in the right amount out of the generosity of your heart. Per dollar spent, you get a lot more satisfaction from spending for the benefit of other people than for yourself. Beware, however, of gifts given with strings attached. Needing approval presented in the guise of generosity is awkward and will not make anyone feel very good.

Give of your time. Your time and attention can be the greatest gift of all. Devoting even a few moments of your time to a person says that you care and is usually greatly appreciated. Volunteering for charitable work makes it clear to yourself and others that the cause is meaningful. With children, spending time is especially important, as children learn most from the example of adults they see every day.

The overwhelming evidence about money is that acquiring money does not make people happier except for those whose financial need is great. Giving it away provides much longer-lasting satisfaction.

Case history: In my parents' home, it was understood

that generosity, especially to those less fortunate, was not optional. This is consistent with Jewish tradition of *tsedakah*, the Hebrew word associated with charity that actually means justice as in a higher justice for all. When my children were growing up, we had a *tsedakah* box in the house into which they were to put a quarter every week from their allowance so they'd get in the habit. We used the money to buy food for a local food bank.

Tsedakah is understood as helping God to heal or perfect the created world. It is so central to a Jew's religious obligations that the Talmud, the ancient code of laws, says, "Even one who receives *tsedakah* should give *tsedakah*." The implication is that even those who are suffering have the obligation to participate in making the world a better place via some kind of sacrifice for the benefit of others. It's a satisfying feeling as well.

Evidence: Elizabeth Dunn, Lara Aknin and Michael Norton looked into the degree to which how people spent money affected their overall happiness. They found that, "spending more of one's income on others predicted greater happiness..." and "even those who were randomly assigned to spend money on others experienced greater happiness than those assigned to spend money on themselves."[30]

The materialistic pursuit of wealth proved less fulfilling than a more generous approach to life. Tim Kasser of Knox College studied three kinds of attitudes about money: frugality, generosity and materialism in children and adolescents. He found that generosity was associated with more happiness and higher self-esteem. Materialism aligned with lower happiness and self-esteem, and more anxiety.[31]

Arthur C. Brooks of the American Enterprise Institute found that generosity increased both happiness *and* income. "Donors ended up with more income after making their gifts... Giving stimulated prosperity." The link between the two is a sense of self-efficacy, according to Brooks, so that generous people felt more in control of their lives and better able to be successful in other ways. Generosity provided a link between two otherwise unrelated aspects of their lives, their material wealth and their sincere convictions. In supporting causes they believe in they found more meaning and greater happiness.[32]

10 Write about your Feelings

While thoughts are linear, moving from one idea or subject to the next, feelings are fluid, more like waves on the ocean. During periods of feeling badly, the fluidity of emotion makes it harder to get to the root of sad feelings and process emotional pain. Often people ruminate, going over and over the internal storms with no way to let them go and move on.

Writing about painful feelings helps. Putting them down as best you can, either on paper or on a computer screen, orders events in time and space by adding structure. The emotions in your gut acquire a form when you give them over to words. Also, once you've written your feelings down you have to some degree released them. You've turned them over to the page where they are less likely to torment you.

Writing about good feelings is beneficial too, though in a different way. When you write down how happy you feel, the act of writing carves the happy sensation in stone. The written declaration of how good you feel becomes a testament to the pleasant emotion, something to cherish even if you never read it again.

Case history: On days when I'm feeling a little off and don't know exactly why, writing feelings down is usually the quickest and most effective thing I can do to regain emotional balance. I have a dedicated notebook in which I may write a single paragraph or more than a page about feelings and related thoughts. My only rule is that I don't know what I'm going to say next, just write. The writing may happen several times in a week or not for a month. Sooner or later I know there will be a moment of emotional uncertainty when free-association writing is the best way to get back on track. It always helps.

Evidence: James W. Pennebaker of Southern Methodist University is the leading researcher on writing about feelings. He concludes, "Extensive research has revealed that when people put their emotional upheavals into words, their physical and mental health improves markedly." Research subjects were asked to write about their deepest thoughts and feelings about traumatic experiences for 15 minutes a day over the course of four consecutive days. The results were striking. "The writing exercise improved their physical health, resulted in better grades, and often changed their lives."[33]

Stephen J. Lepore & Joshua M. Smyth's book, *The Writing Cure: How expressive writing promotes health and emotional well-being* presents a rigorous exploration of how writing feelings down has such salutary effects.[34]

11 Go for a Walk

Walking gets the juices flowing. The feeling of being emotionally stuck that accompanies times of low mood or conflict breaks up with the rhythm of a brisk walk. If problems with other people are what's upsetting you, even a short walk gets you away at least temporarily into a space defined by your own activity and pace. The change of environment can be even more beneficial than the physical exercise.

Outside walking is best, as it exposes you to fresh air and an ongoing change of scenery. When taking a walk outdoors is not possible, indoor walking or climbing stairs also has a beneficial effect. If you are feeling especially stressed, imagine that at every step the unpleasant feeling flows out the bottoms of your feet and into the ground.

Walking by yourself provides time to think matters through without distractions. You will find you are less inclined to ruminate when moving than you would be sitting still. Walking with another person offers the added benefit of socializing, another happiness booster.

Case history: Steve Jobs, the legendary founder of Apple Computers, was known to work through especially thorny problems on long walks. Walking helped clear his mind and relax him, and he did it frequently. Jobs used to go for long walks and deep, meaningful conversations with Larry Ellison, CEO of Oracle, near their Silicon Valley homes.[35]

Walking meetings are becoming popular in business as a better way to work and keep people mentally and emotionally engaged. Amy Buckner Chowdhry, CEO of AnswerLab writing in INC. Magazine, cited walking meetings as a more productive alternative to sitting meetings, as well as a way to keep everyone more fit.[36]

Evidence: British researchers Simona Rasciute and Paul Downward found that physical activity such as walking and cycling improve both health and self-reported well-being.[37] Going for a walk can be helpful in reducing feelings of depression, as Dr. Michal Artal et. al. write: "Physical activity is a useful tool for preventing and easing depression symptoms... A feasible, flexible, and pleasurable program has the best chance for success. Walking—alone or in a group—is often a good option."[38] Rodale News, the health magazine publisher, cites benefits of walking in addition to weight control, as reduced risk of heart disease and stroke, improved insulin sensitivity which reduces the risk of diabetes and maybe even an improved sex life.[39]

12 Enjoy the Present

Right here, right now, is the only time that exists. Putting your attention on the perceptions of your five senses and the moment-to-moment workings of your mind will, in times of distress, make you feel better. Eckhart Tolle, the spiritual teacher, says, "Always say 'yes' to the present moment... Surrender to what is. Say 'yes' to life—and see how life starts suddenly working for you rather than against you."

Engage with the present moment by focusing on senses rather than thoughts. What are the colors and shapes before your eyes right now? What smell in the air can you detect? Can you feel your seat where it touches the chair and the clothes draped across your shoulders?

You could catalog all these sensations continuously as they shift around, but of course an active mind will not allow that. In short order you are back thinking about what happened or how you feel or something else. Still, at any moment, if only for a moment, you can put your attention on this moment and how your senses perceive it.

Focusing on the here and now is called mindfulness and includes paying attention to the workings of your mind as well as your physical senses. Andrew Weill, M.D., defines mindfulness as, "the self-regulation of attention and the ability to maintain attention on one's experience in the present moment."[40]

Mindfulness is a time-honored meditative tradition that has become popular in business. Whether you have ever meditated or not, using the technique of mindfulness to calm the mind and relax the body even in small doses works. It stops hurtful thoughts, unwinds rumination and grows self-awareness. It is accessible at any moment, often best accompanied by one or more deep breaths. If you have never practiced mindfulness, try it in small doses to soften a moment's tension. Even a few seconds of rest from painful thoughts or feelings makes your life a tiny bit happier.

Case history: Walking in a bustling city lends itself to practicing mindfulness. When I lived in New York City I would occasionally do that while out in various neighborhoods. I tried to notice every sight, sound and smell with full attention and always had a marvelous time. There was so much to observe in every direction. The shapes, the colors, the noise of traffic and pedestrians absorbed me completely and I felt especially safe. At the same time, I found it relaxing because my full attention was on everything "out there" so that I forgot about myself and my concerns, at least for a little while.

Evidence: A leading researcher on mindfulness is Ellen Langer of Harvard, who describes ordinary mindfulness as, "...a state of alertness and lively awareness."[41] A description of her book *Mindfulness* says, "When we are mindful, we are open to surprise, oriented in the present moment, sensitive to context, and above all, liberated from the tyranny of old mindsets."

Jon Kabat-Zinn, PhD, has taught mindfulness to reduce stress for years. His best-selling book is *Full*

Catastrophe Living: Using the Wisdom of Your Body and Mind to Face Stress, Pain and Illness. Mindfulness practice has even been shown to help sufferers achieve significant reduction in physical pain.[42]

Which of these 12 keys appeal to you most? Which do you think will be most effective for you? *Which one will you try right now?* Remember that to get the benefit you need to take action and keep at it.

These twelve keys address your immediate feelings. Strategies to help you become happier tomorrow and for the rest of your life are in the next chapter.

7

12 More for a Better Tomorrow

This chapter is the payoff: twelve specific actions for you to try to grow your emotional well-being, to become happier, over months and years. Every one is supported by documentation, the evidence: you can trust that they are valid. Of course, you can't do them all at once. Choose a couple that appeal most to you and get started. Integrate them into your daily routine. Over time you should try as many of them as you can.

From where we are at any moment, it may be hard to imagine exactly what a happier life would look like. But we can imagine that it could be better than today, even if today is reasonably good. There is no upper limit. Every step in the right direction is worthwhile. Bad things will still happen, of course, and there will still be setbacks and loss. The aim is to increase the overall quality of your life experience. You can do this. These twelve keys will help.

1 Lighten Up

Do you ever laugh at yourself, your overblown ideas or your human foibles? If you don't, if you never find yourself even a little foolish, you could be taking yourself way too seriously. Lighten up! Be serious-minded about what you do, but don't take yourself so seriously.

We all think we're important. And we *are* to ourselves and a small circle of friends and family. We are not nearly as important to everyone else. The great majority of people we know, even those who like us, would live pretty much the same were we to suddenly vanish.

Taking ourselves too seriously is a burden. It undermines the simple pleasures of daily life and hurts our ability to roll with the ups and downs that are inevitable for everyone. Most of us fall into this trap sometimes, especially between our teenage years and our thirties. For some, it never stops. If you find yourself wrapped up in self-seriousness, stop for a moment. Soften the thinking about yourself and look around you. Take a deep breath and smile. It will make you feel more relaxed and probably less tired at the end of the day. You can do it again and again.

All this suggests that one way to be happier is to back off intense focus on yourself and how you're doing, and lighten up. Frequently.

Evidence: Trying too hard to make everything perfect may be easier to recognize in how we treat our children than ourselves. Alvin Rosenfeld M.D. and Nicole Wise write in *Hyper-Parenting: Are You Hurting Your Child by Trying Too Hard?:* "We well-meaning mothers and fathers worry about matters big and small, striving to micromanage every detail of our kids' lives... Wouldn't it be a good idea to let our kids have their turn, so they can learn and grow from the good and not-so-good experiences in their lives?" The book contains examples of parents trying to turn their children into superstars instead of letting them be children. The explicit message of the book is to lighten up on parenting for the good of the children. Implicit is that parents will be better off if they lighten up on their own lives too.

Gestalt therapist Barry Stevens (1902 – 1985) conveyed the idea of not trying too hard all the time elegantly in the title of her book *Don't Push the River: It Flows by Itself.*

2 Socialize with Friends More

Enjoying the company of friends is an easy strategy to building a happier life. You get together to talk, play or eat, and everyone goes home happier.

Make the time to enjoy your friends. Stay in touch and plan to get together, especially if you haven't in a while. Pay special attention to old friends. If you've stayed friends for years, there is a good reason. When you cannot get together in person, call them to talk. Socializing through the Internet is better than none at all. Don't take important friend relationships for granted. Even strongly felt friendships can weaken beyond repair if you neglect them for too long.

Choose friends who are happy people to the degree you can. Joy is contagious. The fun of laughing with cheerful people far exceeds any benefit from commiserating with a pessimistic crowd. A story in the Huffington Post reports from the Framingham Heart Study that "those who are surrounded by happy people are more likely to become happy in the future."[43]

Socializing is less about the content of the conversation and more about the shared experience of being alive. If you don't have enough friends, make the effort to find new ones. The Internet makes it easier than ever to find others who care about what you care about and like what you like. Look especially for people you can meet in person.

Evidence: "The good life is built with good relationships" concludes the Harvard Study of Adult Development according to its director, Robert Waldinger.[44] Over the 75 years of the study, close personal relationships and good friendships proved to be the strongest predictor of longevity and better physical health in old age.

"Solid scientific evidence shows that social relationships affect a range of health outcomes, including mental health, physical health, health habits, and mortality risk" concludes a meta-study by Debra Umberson and Jennifer Montez.[45] Even accounting for socio-economic factors, "Adults who are more socially connected are healthier and live longer than their more isolated peers." Those with low levels of social engagement tend to be sicker and die younger.

Andrew Weil, M.D. asserts that social isolation, a

common outgrowth of contemporary life, is bad for us. He recounts moving from a rural home to a town and being happier for it. He writes, "If you want to be in optimum emotional health, realize that social isolation stands between you and it… Join groups, find communities, whatever. Spontaneous happiness is incompatible with social isolation. Period."[46]

3 Cultivate the Spiritual

The words "spiritual" and "religious" mean different things to different people. Yet the impulse to connect with something beyond our own selves on a deeper level, whatever you call it, appears to be all but universal.

Consider that every culture around the world has generated some version of religion, creating deities to explain natural phenomena, discovering God, or simply feeling a sense of alignment with what that lies beyond our ability to comprehend. Eric Weiner, author of *The Geography of Bliss*, concludes from his investigation of happiness in ten countries around the world, "An important ingredient in the good life, the happy life, is connecting to something larger than ourselves."[47]

Belief in God or a Higher Power is a common path to such understanding, but not the only way. Some find it in the appreciation of Nature or the arts. Some find it through science, at the limits of what can be known and measured. For many, the spiritual is a by-product of the experience of love.

What meaningful spiritual connection amplifies your inner life? If you don't have one, you might do some exploration. You don't have to accept the religion your parents taught you. What speaks to you spiritually may change over the course of years as the relationship with the sacred evolves. Cultivation of the spiritual also reinforces other healthy behaviors such as gratitude, compassion and generosity.

Evidence: Step two of the twelve steps of Alcoholics Anonymous and other 12-step programs says, "Came to believe that a Power greater than ourselves would restore us to sanity." Participants in such programs talk at length about the critical role their Higher Power plays in their recovery. Through alignment with something outside themselves—many refer explicitly to God though many others understand Higher Power differently—those who have suffered from uncontrollable harmful habits have straightened out their lives. Anecdotally, those who start in such programs and cannot find some version of the Higher Power have a harder time staying sober.

Ellen L. Idler PhD of Rutgers University, writing in the Spirituality in Higher Education Newsletter, says that spiritual experiences "lift us up out of our narrow selves and give us a glimpse—if only temporary—of another way to view things as a part, however small, of a larger picture. Spiritual and religious practices that help us integrate the body, mind, and spirit, also provide psychological and physical benefits, as research from the past two decades has shown."[48]

4 Engage in Work that is Meaningful

"Work is love made visible," said Khalil Gibran in his classic book, *The Prophet*. Work that is meaningful organizes your activity around what matters to you, so that your efforts lead to greater satisfaction and happiness.

"Work" is what you put effort into in order to achieve a result, as opposed to leisure activity done for its own sake. It can be a paying job, a business, artistic pursuit, caretaking or some other activity. Raising children is the work of many parents, both women and men. Volunteer work, political organizing, religious engagement can all be principal work we do for a known purpose.

Meaningful work aligns with your personal values and helps you bring more of what you care about into the world. You feel that your effort is worthwhile, that it makes a positive difference. Contrast that to work that has no meaning or in which you can find no meaning at all. You would be going through empty motions. While a job that pays the bills can be very valuable, in the long run you are best off if you can choose work and a career that rewards you with the sense that your time and labor are generating something worthwhile.

The meaning in your work may arise not from the task itself but from how you interpret it. Many ordinary jobs serve valuable ends that are not immediately visible. And many working people create meaning in their jobs by how they understand what they do. Positive psychology teacher Tal ben-Shahar tells of a banker in his native Israel who arranges mortgages for homeowners. After decades of approving loans, she seemed overwhelmingly happy with her work. When asked why, she said, "I help people achieve their dreams."[49]

What is meaningful to you about work you do? How might you understand it to make it more so? If you cannot find meaning, a sense that what you are doing is important, perhaps it is time to find other work that will satisfy you more.

Evidence: Work, both paid and not paid, consumes such a large portion of people's lives that it cannot help being a factor in overall happiness. Ivan Robertson and Cary Cooper explore the relationship between work and happiness in their book, *Well-Being, Productivity and Happiness at Work* that says, "Work that is rewarding, involving good relationships with colleagues and opportunities to feel a sense of achievement on a regular basis, is a key factor in psychological well-being."[50]

Professor Martin Seligman, the founder of the positive psychology field, asserts, "Human beings, ineluctably, want meaning and purpose in life."[51] He defines meaning as "belonging to and serving something that you believe is bigger than the self"[52] and includes it among the five essential components of human flourishing. (The other four are positive emotion, engagement, relationships and accomplishment.) As much time as we spend at work, it is critical to our well-being that our efforts have some kind of meaning.

5 Participate in Rituals

Ritual actions add order and comfort as well as meaning to daily life. A ritual is any action you do deliberately the same, consistently over a period of time. Rituals include religious practices, holidays, reunions, annual parties, personal daily activities and other intentional actions reinforced by repetition.

Daily prayer or meditation is a ritual, as is making a to-do list in the morning. Reading before bed, going to the gym, keeping a journal or calling your parents every Sunday are ritual actions as are sharing Thanksgiving with family or spending a week at the beach every summer. When you perform these actions, you get a double benefit, first from actions themselves and second from the reinforcement of doing them repeatedly.

Rituals share the important characteristic of continuity with habits, those extremely powerful patterns that make life so much more manageable because you don't have to figure out how to do things each time. The difference is that habits, both good ones and bad ones, seem to grow up by themselves while rituals are those you intentionally engage in based on what you care about.

Every community has annual rituals—seasonal, memorial or just made-up fun ones—that are enjoyable to participate in. Find the ones you like and do as many as you care to.

You can also create new rituals that are unique to you. When my children were young we used to commemorate each new season with a visit to the woods behind the house where we'd celebrate the budding of spring, the lush green of summer, the colors of autumn, or the bare trees and snow of winter. These "season-fests", as we called them, became a meaningful ritual to our family and may well become part of my daughters' families' lives as well.

To create your own rituals, find an activity that speaks to your heart, make up an appropriate action and schedule when to perform it. Once you get into a groove of doing it for a while, the action starts to feel normal. Eventually the ritual becomes important enough that you won't want to miss it. My morning ritual includes a cup of tea, a few minutes of sitting in silence, followed by a detailed vision of one thing I especially want to happen. It works for me, as one that you create can work for you. After a few years of doing this, when I miss a day I feel the difference.

Personal story: When I was in my 20's and feeling a failure, I created a ritual for myself. Every night I'd write on a pad of paper "10 successes of the day" and make a list. Some days the list contained important achievements. Other days my accomplishments were so meager that brushing my teeth as planned counted as a success.

I did it every night. If I'd gone to bed without listing ten successes and was almost asleep, I'd get up, turn on the light, and write. After a while I stopped thinking about what I was doing and why.

I did this for six or eight months. One day, for no particular reason, I noticed that I did not feel like a failure anymore. That nagging feeling was gone. It had lifted. I quit making the list. Through good and bad times since, the awful feeling of being a failure has not returned.

Evidence: Rituals work best when they are specific

actions planned and done at specific times. Jim Loehr and Tony Schwartz in *The Power of Full Engagement* found that following well-designed ritual actions led to better performance in sports and in business than relying on self-discipline alone. Their key to generating effective rituals is that they be "motivated by deeply held values."[53]

One need only look at how effective religious rituals are at bringing comfort and a feeling of well-being to those who attend collective worship. The rituals of the service, done the same way every time, strengthen a worshipper's sense of identity in the faith. Changing these rituals or interrupting their regularity would be profoundly upsetting.

6 Set Goals and Strive to Achieve Them

Aspiration focuses your attention forward and makes you happier. Goals organize thinking and engage emotion. Making plans to achieve your goals, especially with other people, is a simple happiness-enhancing strategy that has the added benefit of actually getting you closer to what you want.

Commitment to a goal is a message to ourselves and others that we intend to accomplish something even in the face of obstacles. Working to achieve a vision of a better future—the goal—energizes us. Planning gets the juices flowing as we look into the specifics of how to get from here to there. This leads to enthusiasm, a powerful life force. Imagining the full realization of your goals generates hope, a strong positive emotion. Even if you are not certain you will succeed, simply picturing what you want and committing yourself to it adds momentum.

While failure is possible in any significant undertaking, holding back because you fear failure is a mistake. The pain associated with the fear of failure is worse than the pain of actually failing. Taking your lumps may be exactly what you need to learn what it takes to succeed the next time.

People typically have a whole range of goals, easy and hard ones, short term ones and those that may take many years. As you write down your goals, and you must write them not just think them, be sure to include goals of varying time frames and importance. Achieving the easier ones will support the pursuit of the harder ones. Put your written list somewhere you will see it and read it over often.

Evidence: There is a host of research that supports making and pursuing goals as a happiness-enhancing activity. Mihaly Csikszentmihalyi's work on flow asserts that total engagement in goal-directed activity makes people happier. He says, "The way to improve the quality of life is not primarily through thinking but through doing. The issue is not to figure out how to be happy, satisfied or contented, but to act in ways that will bring about those states of experience directly."[54]

Do some kinds of goals make you happier than others? Kennon Sheldon and Andrew Elliott recommend "self-concordant" goals, those that are consistent with a person's overall interests and core values, as beneficial in two ways: "First, those pursuing self-concordant goals put more sustained effort into achieving those goals and thus are more likely to attain them. Second, those who attain self-concordant goals reap greater well-being benefits from their attainment."[55]

7 Spend Money on Activities and People rather than Things

When has a new thing ever made you happy for long? Even new cars—very expensive things—are thrilling only for a short while. Within days or weeks, the excitement of the car's novelty is gone even if we continue to enjoy using it. Yet those car commercials that bombard the television never stop pushing the message that a new car will make you happy.

Psychologists call it "hedonic adaptation" the tendency for the new to lose its luster quickly. Even newfound wealth stops being emotionally rewarding in short order, much to the dismay of many lottery winners. You see hedonic adaptation with children who get new toys and adults with the latest electronic gadgets. The thing stays the same but the satisfaction associated with it fades.

Activities are different. Because activities happen through time, they engage ongoing attention. They can't get old. Whether it's a wonderful dinner or a trip to Paris, the pleasure of an active experience is in the doing.

If you look back at the memorable pleasures of your life, you would be remembering activities and experiences and probably the people you did them with. Almost never would a physical object stand out as a lingering source of happiness. That should tell you something. If you want to create more pleasures, invest in activities and people, not things.

This principle applies to gift giving as well. If you are wondering what gift to buy someone, consider giving an experience rather than an object, especially for someone who already has many possessions. Tickets to a sporting event or concert or a day at a wonderful outdoor activity are likely to be received more joyously than something off the shelf at the gift store. Activity gifts show that you've thought about what that person enjoys and made an effort to please him or her. It feels more personal.

Here are two hints to making the pleasure of experiences even better. First, share them with people you like. Any good activity shared is more pleasurable. Second, if you want the memory of the activity to be positive, arrange for the ending to be especially good. You will remember pleasure from the last day of the vacation better than any other day. Plan ahead to make sure longer activities and experiences end on a high note so that they reside more happily in memory.

Evidence: "...once our basic needs are met, acquiring more possessions—bigger, better, newer, shinier—doesn't make us any happier. At most it gives us a temporary high, similar to addicts' getting their fix." Says psychologist and author Tal ben-Shahar.[56]

Leonardo Nicolao et. al. found that people adapt more slowly to experiential purchases than material purchases, which explains why the enjoyment of activities provides longer lasting satisfaction.[57]

8 Exercise Both the Physical and the Mental

Everyone knows exercise is good for your physical health. Aerobic and resistance-based exercise strengthens the body, helps you control your weight and increases the chance of a longer, healthier life.

Exercise is good for your mental health as well. It helps reduce stress and anxiety and is an antidote to depression. Andrew Weil, M.D., says that regular exercise "is such a key component of a healthy lifestyle...integrative exercise is good for both mind and body, and getting regular exercise both prevents and relieves mood problems."[58]

Find a type of exercise that is right for you, and at the right level. Are sports and games better than working out at the gym or swimming? If you have trouble getting started, find someone else to start with, even if it's just going for a chatty morning walk, and move on from there.

Mental exercise is important too. Using your brain to think and imagine makes you feel more alive and engaged. You don't have to be especially intellectual or have academic training. Exercise your brain by thinking deeply about topics that interest you and pursue them in serious conversation with others.

Commit to continued learning. Try something new. Many colleges offer classes to the public at reasonable cost on subjects that help build careers or are just for fun. Online learning opportunities continue to grow, including classes taught by top professors. New learning can be thrilling and a welcome respite from a repetitive work. Open your mind through lifelong learning, develop new skills, enjoy wonders that are within your reach.

Read, especially books both fiction and non-fiction. Books exercise your mind and your imagination, make you smarter and better able to cope with change. They get you into the depths of ideas instead of skimming across the surface as with a short news article on the Internet or TV. Fiction books give you the pleasure of immersing yourself in an imagined world that surely has some bearing on your own. Non-fiction books provide new learning to engage your mind as you grow through life. If you want to learn more about positive psychology, pick up some of the books listed in the bibliography.

Most of us will live at least into our 70's or 80's. By exercising both the body and the mind continually at every stage we are much more likely to reach our later years healthy and feeling alive in body, mind and spirit.

Evidence: Bonnie G. Berger, writing in the journal Quest about the psychological benefits of an active lifestyle, says: "Planned and structured physical activity is associated with psychological benefits in four broad areas: enhanced mood, stress reduction, a more positive self-concept and a higher quality of life."[59]

Sonja Lyubomirsky cites a study by Blumenthal et. al. where clinically depressed older patients were treated either with anti-depressant medication or a program of aerobic exercise or both. The exercise program proved equally effective to the medication in lifting the depression at lower cost and with fewer side-effects, and kept subjects from relapsing into their depression longer.[60]

Mahncke et. al. showed that a program of brain training reduced age-related cognitive decline in mature adults.[61]

9 Be Curious

Curiosity wakes up your mind and makes you feel more alive. When you are curious you want to know more, see more, taste more of what life has to offer.

Everything you know about virtually any subject is incomplete. If you are curious, you can discover more. At the same time, it's all but impossible to worry about ourselves and our problems when caught up in curious engagement.

Some people seem to be born curious. Others learn it during their upbringing and education. For the rest of us, curiosity is easy to pick up. Ask questions of people who know better than you do. What is beyond your current knowledge on any topic, and why? What interested you as a child or in school? There is so much to learn. Pursue new discovery and you will feel more engaged, more enthusiastic and happier.

Evidence: Stanford professor Carol Dweck, in her book *Mindset*, distinguishes the *growth* mindset from the *fixed* mindset. In the growth mindset, one is constantly learning, engaged and growing. Growth mindset people eagerly absorb what life has to offer them. They see failure, in almost anything, as an opportunity to learn and prepare to do better the next time. They are constantly discovering more about themselves and the world they live in. They hunger to learn and find joy in discovery. By contrast, fixed mindset people sit back and judge. They find fault with others, and themselves, easily. They assume they can't change, and that assumption usually turns out to be self-fulfilling.[62]

Todd Kashdan and Michael Steger reported on the connection between curiosity and happiness: "We found that...people high in trait curiosity reported more frequent growth-oriented behaviors, and greater presence of meaning, search for meaning, and life satisfaction."[63]

10 Appreciate and be Grateful

Every time you appreciate someone or something you feel a moment of good feeling. Appreciating anything: a person, some aspect of your life, even the weather, brings you into the present moment and is one of the simplest things you can do to feel better. Appreciation of what is good in your life is a habit to cultivate that leads to more and more good feelings. Tal ben-Shahar, author of *Happier*, is fond of saying, "If you appreciate the good, the good appreciates."

Notice the good things in your life and acknowledge how much they mean to you. Savor them and be grateful. Appreciate good health, good friends and family, the place where you live, your favorite music, feeling safe in the world. Stop for a moment and be grateful that you can afford to feed yourself or that you live in a free country.

It is so easy to take these things for granted. But taking them for granted is a mistake that diminishes happiness. Instead, get in the habit of stopping frequently to recognize the goodness in your own life and what that means to you.

Could you find something to gripe about? Of course. You always have a choice to focus on the good or the bad. But focusing on the bad brings only misery or at best some sympathy. People who complain all the time are no fun to be with. Is that how you want people to see you?

To be happier over the long term, develop an intentional

attitude of gratitude. It takes but a few moments and yields lasting positive results. Sonja Lyubomirsky describes gratitude as "a kind of metastrategy for achieving happiness...a neutralizer of envy, avarice, hostility, worry and irritation."[64] Who wouldn't want that?

The benefits of feeling grateful are reinforced by thanking others. Thanking someone for a kindness done on your behalf accomplishes two things. First, the other person gets to feel good because everyone likes to be thanked. Second, you get to feel good because offering thanks is an appreciative happiness-inducing act.

Evidence: Robert Emmons of the University of California at Davis says, "Gratitude is literally one of the few things that can measurably change people's lives... The evidence on gratitude contradicts the widely held view that people have a 'set-point' of happiness that cannot be reset by any known means."[65]

Alex M. Wood et. al conclude: "Gratitude...is uniquely important to psychological well-being."[66] This phenomenon is not limited to American or Western culture. A study of student athletes in Taiwan showed that those athletes who approached their participation with an attitude of gratefulness were happier teammates and less likely to suffer burnout.[67]

11 Serve Others

Being of service to other people is immensely rewarding. That is true about looking after people you love and also true about helping people you've never met. An act of service brings out the best in all of us.

What serving others looks like is entirely up to you. Many programs already exist, such as tutoring children or serving food at a soup kitchen, but volunteer work in the community is only one option. Serving others can be as small as giving up your seat on the bus to an elderly person to as large as starting your own not-for-profit organization to make the world a better place. If you belong to a formal religious organization service options are likely already available to you.

Participating personally is the most satisfying kind of service. You become engaged with people whose needs are greater than yours. A meaningful reward of service work is in making a personal connection with other people, a root experience of positive emotion.[68] You might also find that those in need are much more similar to you than you might have imagined, which gives a deeper perspective on our shared humanity.

Serving others can be addicting. If you've found a vehicle to perform service that suits your style and temperament, you'll probably want to do it on a regular basis. It's that satisfying. If service fails to provide such gratification, chances are you've chosen the wrong kind of service project. Try something else. Though we all appreciate being thanked, we cannot do service just for the thanks we might or might not receive.

How is doing service a key to happiness? It feels meaningful in the sense of contributing to something larger than ourselves. Another important benefit of performing service to others is that it gets our attention off ourselves. Since we can only feel badly when we are thinking about ourselves, focusing on others shifts our perspective. The best moments in life happen when we are focused externally with virtually no attention on us and how we are doing. Engagement in service to others provides such moments and adds meaning, and often love, to our busy lives.

The newsletter for a shelter organization I support says, "The best way to find yourself is to lose yourself in service to others."

Evidence: A study by Peggy Thoits and Lyndi Hewitt of Vanderbilt University into the effects of performing volunteer work concludes, "...volunteer work...enhances all six aspects of well-being...happiness, life satisfaction, self esteem, sense of control over life, physical health and depression."[69]

A study called "Doing Well by Doing Good" by Francesca Borgonovi reports "...people who volunteer report better health and greater happiness than people who do not."[70]

12 Do What you Love

What one or two things do you love to do that make you happy?

All the short-term keys to happiness in Chapter 6 and the longer term ones above are specific, evidence-backed activities that have a proven track record of helping people enjoy life. Yet, many people have their own personal keys to happiness that might not fit in any of these categories.

What's yours? Do you love to fish or do needlework? Have you a favorite activity that is especially pleasurable because you learned it from a grandparent? Is it something you happened on one day that you've enjoyed ever since? What makes your cares drop away and your heart sing just because it's what you love to do?

A survey of activities that bring people joy barely scratches the surface of what's possible. Here are a few:

- Gardening
- Woodworking
- Hiking and camping
- Going to the beach
- Watching movies
- Golf
- Cooking and baking
- Travel to foreign places
- Visiting museums
- Playing a musical instrument
- Dancing
- Singing
- Reading fiction
- Bird watching

- Star gazing
- Concerts and performances of all kinds
- Volunteering in the community
- Spending time with children

Activities such as these are inherently rewarding. You do them because they are fun, and even more fun when you can share them. Look to find others with whom to share your favorite activity. Join a club or group. In the Internet age it is easier than ever to find like-minded people nearby or across the world with whom you can talk about what you enjoy. You might even plan to do it together. What better way to meet people than in sharing an activity you both love?

If you don't immediately have the answer to "What do I love to do?" start by imagining what you might enjoy doing. Explore and try things, especially things that you are naturally good at. Share them when you can. If you still can't find something, talk it out with someone you trust or hire a life coach to help you distill your preferences. All the happiness advice in the world pales in comparison to doing what you love.

Evidence: Martha Beck, a renowned life coach and

author of best-selling books such as *Finding Your Own North Star*, says, "Everything I've ever taught in terms of self-help boils down to this—I cannot believe people keep paying me to say this—if something feels really good for you, you might want to do it. And if it feels really horrible, you might want to consider not doing it."[71]

8

Fear and Courage

You now have at your fingertips proven techniques for increasing your well-being. They have worked for others and they can work for you too. You could expect to begin today and achieve a much happier life soon. That's possible but far from guaranteed. You know from experience how hard change can be. Homeostasis, the automatic resistance to change, gets in the way. An even bigger deterrent is fear.

Fear is almost always the underlying reason when we want to do something important but just can't get around to it. It may feel like laziness or distraction or being too busy. Underneath it's fear, and it stops us in our tracks. We fear failing, losing, looking bad, or disappointing others or ourselves. We rationalize and procrastinate hoping it will go away. We wait until we feel more like it, but waiting for the fear to subside does not work because in most cases the fear never goes away.

Fear when attempting significant change is normal. It's nothing to be ashamed of—everyone you know feels it too. Author Steven Pressfield reminds us that such fear isn't a bad thing, it's actually a helpful sign. It tells us that something is important enough to care about. He says, "If it meant nothing to us, there'd be no [fear]."[72]

When you find yourself putting off actions you know are important, acknowledge the fear lurking inside. Tell yourself, even say out loud, "I feel afraid," even if you don't know of what yet. Admitting to fear brings the hidden emotion into the open so that it loses some of its power.

Then you must act. Replace the thought of whatever you might be afraid of with a picture of the future you desire and take an action step toward it. When? As soon as possible. The longer you delay the harder it gets to act at all.

Nothing breaks down fear like moving forward despite feeling afraid. That's what courage is—taking positive action in the face of fear. Oprah Winfrey tells us to "have the courage to step out of our history and past so that we can live our dreams." Courage is that life-changing, and it's available to anyone. Take action before fear has the chance to stop you. You will get closer to your goal and feel better about yourself too.

I used to carry in my wallet a card with the word COURAGE printed in large letters. When I felt afraid, I'd pull out the card, see that I had courage right there with me, and do things I might otherwise have been too shy, that is, afraid, to do. Try carrying a courage card if it might help you.

You are going to feel afraid sometimes, that is certain. Cultivate courage when the shadow of fear weakens your resolve. Becoming a more courageous person will grow your confidence and boost your sense of well-being.

Do not underestimate what it takes to build a happier life as if it were easy, but don't overestimate the challenges either. Call on your inner strength. Invoke the support of your best allies. Be courageous. Improving the quality of your life is worthy of your time and effort. Many, many people have turned life's difficulties around and you can too. Commit to growing your personal well-being using any and every technique and resource you can find.

Look over the 24 keys from time to time. You never know when one of them, even one you did not think suited you, will be exactly right for the moment. Only you can make your life happier, better, more fulfilling. *You can do this.*

Why not start today? Make the most of your one and only life.

9

If You Can Only Do Three

You now have 24 proven keys to creating a happier life both today and tomorrow. I hope you will use at least some of them. If all this feels like too much and you aren't sure where to start, here are three you can definitely do that will make a noticeable difference.

1 Keep a Gratitude Notebook.

Every night after dinner or before you go to bed, write down five things you are grateful for today. Include anything that happened that you are glad of, even if you don't feel especially grateful. You will learn to feel that. If five is too many, write three. If that is beyond your ability to commit to, write one. Every day.

What you are grateful for can be large or small. Even very small things count. You can be grateful that the weather was pleasant or you got home safely. It is perfectly acceptable to write the same one frequently, even every day. When I think of what I am grateful for, at the top of my list is that my daughter, who nearly died some years ago, is alive.

A gratitude notebook is private. You don't even have to tell anyone you are doing it. During the day you might find that you enjoy thinking about what you will write that night. It's not nearly as effective just to think about what you are grateful for. Write it down. If you miss a day or longer just start again.

I recommend you keep a gratitude notebook for at least six months.

2 Perform a Deliberate Act of Kindness for Another Person Every Day.

Commit in the morning to finding some occasion when you can exhibit kindness to someone. It can be a person you know or a stranger, and the act can be visible or not. You may or may not be thanked for it, or even noticed. What's important is that it feels like an act of kindness that you intentionally choose to do for another human being every day.

Marty Seligman, the founder of positive psychology,

says, "Doing a kindness produces the single most reliable momentary increase in well-being of any exercise we have tested."[73] It's best if you vary how you fulfill this step. Do different actions for different people, and do at least one every day.

3 Seek Out The Company of People You Care About and Socialize.

Recent positive psychology research has emphasized interpersonal relationships as an abiding factor in long-term well-being. The social element is that important in providing the fertile soil in which contentment can grow.

They don't all have to be close friends. Acquaintances are enjoyable to spend time with too. Don't be afraid to strike up a conversation with people you don't know. Many people have rewarding short conversations with complete strangers on buses and in bars.

If you lack enough community, make the effort to make new friends. Look for what you have in common with others—children, favorite activities, local sports teams—and talk about that. Identify people you are drawn to and start to build a friendship. If you have family members you like nearby, visit with them. Friends from the past can be wonderful to reconnect with even occasionally.

Even if you are a loner or introvert, there are people whose company you enjoy. Seek them out. It may be harder to build new relationships, especially if you are shy, but it's worth it. If you listen to the words of old people about what has been the most meaningful through the years, you'll usually hear about personal relationships. Start building them now.

These three are a good place to start. Do them and you *will* feel a difference.

10

Being True to Yourself

As you embark on the journey to build a happier life, using the keys presented here, there is one underlying principle that will help all your efforts succeed.

Be true to yourself.

Being true to yourself means living with integrity, a moral consistency that infuses everything you do. It is not a specific set of actions. It is a way of behaving that governs all your actions and all your relationships. Being true to yourself makes you whole at the deepest level.

It starts with self knowledge. We come to know ourselves through introspection, reflection, conversation and seeing how others respond to us. Discovering the inner self can take a long time—perhaps even a lifetime. It's worth the effort. Eventually we settle on certain core principles and values. Being true to yourself means applying those principles and values consistently.

The centrality of being true to yourself as a recipe for a good life dates back to Greek philosopher Aristotle in the 4th century BCE. Aristotle spoke of *Eudaimonia*, truth to one's inner self. "According to this view, happiness entails identifying one's virtues, cultivating them, and living in accordance with them."[74]

Compromising what you know is right may bring short-term rewards. But every time you betray your values you diminish the relationship with yourself. If your long-term goal is to be satisfied with your life, you must be able to look in the mirror and be at peace with the person you see. If you can't be at peace with you, every other relationship will suffer. When you are at peace with you, all your relationships benefit.

Being true to yourself as much as possible gives you a firm foundation on which to build greater happiness. Without it something will always be missing. Start today to be true to yourself in every moment you can. It is the single most powerful thing you can do to create a happier life.

Notes

1. Ricard, Matthieu, *Happiness* 194/320*
2. Haidt, Jonathan, *the Happinerss Hypothesis,* p.90
3. Ricard, Ibid 229/320
4. Lyubomirsky, Sonia, *The How of Happiness*, p.5
5. Rath & Harter, *The Five Elements of Wellbeing*, Gallup Business Journal, May 4, 2010
6. Sarasen et. al., *Assessing Social Support*, Journal of Personality and Social Psychology, Jan. 1983
7. Locke & Latham, *New Directions in Goal-setting theory,* Current Directions in Psychological Science, Oct. 2006
8. Laird, James D., Journal of Personality and Social Psychology, Vol. 29(4), Apr 1974
9. Pugh, S. Douglas, *Service with a Smile: Emotional Contagion in the Service Encounter,* Academy of Management Journal, Oct. 2001
10. Hutcherson, Cendri, et. al. *Loving-kindness meditation increases social connectedness*, Emotion, Vol. 8, Issue 5, 2008
11. Kahneman, Daniel, *Thinking Fast and Slow*, p. 395
12. Diener and Seligman, Psychological Science, Jan. 2002
13. Epictetus: http://plato.stanford.edu/entries/epictetus/
14. Carson, Shelley H. and Langer, Ellen J., *Mindfulness and Self-acceptance,* Journal of Rational-Emotive and Cognitive-Behavior Therapy, March 2006, Volume 24
15. Chamberlain, John and Haaga, David, *Unconditional Self-Acceptance and Psychological Health*, Journal of Rational-Emotive and Cognitive-Behavior Therapy, September 2001, Vol. 19
16. New York Times, 10/19/2013

---

* Notation xxx/yyy refers to e-books with variable type size, where the lower number is the total number of pages at that size and the upper number the location of the citation

17. Lyubomirsky, Ibid, p.128
18. Layous, Kristin et. al. http://www.plosone.org/article/info%3Adoi%2F10.1371%2Fjournal.pone.0051380
19. Barton, Jo and Pretty, Jules, *What is the Best Dose of Nature and Green Exercise for Improving Mental Health? A Multi-Study Analysis,* Interdisciplinary Centre for Environment and Society, Department of Biological Sciences, University of Essex, Colchester, U.K.
20. MacKerron, George and Mourato, Susana, *Happiness is greater in Natural Environments,* Centre for Advanced Spatial Analysis, University College London, Gower Street, London, UK
21. http://www.onbeing.org/program/the-science-of-healing-places/4856
22. Mongrain, Myriam et. al., *Practicing Compassion Increases Happiness and Self-Esteem,* Journal of Happiness Studies, December, 2011
23. Rigg, Melvin, *The Mood Effects of Music, a Comparison of Data from Four Investigators,* The Journal of Psychology: Interdisciplinary and Applied, 1964
24. Guzzetta, C.E., *Effects of relaxation and music therapy on patients in a coronary care unit with presumptive acute myocardial infarction*, Heart and Lung, the Journal of Critical Care, 1989
25. Bolton, Martha, *The Official Hugs Book*
26. Cohen, Stuart, *The Seventh System,* p.11
27. Clipman, J.M., from a paper presented to the Eastern Psychological Association, Boston, March, 1999
28. Bloom, Howard, *The Lucifer Principle,* Grove/Atlantic, 1995
29. Weisberg, Judith and Haberman, Maxine, Journal of Gerontological Social Work, Vol. 13, 1989
30. Dunn, Aknin & Norton, *Spending Money on Others Promotes Happiness,* Science, March, 2008
31. Kasser, Tim, *What do Children Need to Flourish?,* The Search

Institute Series on Developmentally Attentive Community and Society, Vol. 3, 2005
32. Brooks, Arthur C., New York Times, 3/30/2014
33. Pennebaker, James W. and Seagel, Jane D., *Forming a Story: the Health Benefits of Narrative (for E.)*, Journal of Clinical Psychology, Oct. 1999
34. Lepore, Stephen and Smyth, Joshua, American Psychological Association, 2002
35. Isaacson, Walter, *Steve Jobs*, Simon & Schuster, 2012, 406/1584
36. http://www.inc.com/amy-buckner/walk-and-talks-more-productive-than-your-think.html
37. Rasciute, Simona and Downward, Paul, *Health or Happiness? What is the Impact of Physical Activity on the Individual?*, Kyklos, Vol. 63, May, 2010
38. Artal, Michal et. al., *Exercise against Depression,* The Physician and Sportsmedicine, Vol. 26, Issue 10, 1998
39. http://www.rodalenews.com/benefits-walking
40. Weil, Andrew M.D., *Spontaneous Happiness,* p.66
41. Langer, Ellen, *Minding Matters, the consequences of mindlessness-mindfulness.*, Advances in Experimental Social Psychology, Vol. 22, Academic Press, 1989
42. Kabat-Zinn, Jon, *An outpatient program in behavioral medicine for chronic pain patients based on the practice of mindfulness meditation,* General Hospital Psychiatry, Vol. 4, April 1982
43. *The Habits of Supremely Happy People,* Huffington Post, 9/16/2013
44. http://www.ted.com/talks/robert_waldinger_what_makes_a_good_life_lessons_from_the_longest_study_on_happiness
45. Umberson, Debra and Montez, Jennifer, *Social Relationships and Health,* Journal of Health and Social Behavior, November, 2010
46. Weil, Ibid p.165

47. Weiner, Eric, *The Geography of Bliss,* 138/405
48. Idler, Ellen L., *The Psychological and Physical Benefits of Spiritual/Religious Practices,* Spirituality in Higher Education Newsletter, Feb. 2008
49. Lecture in Lenox, MA, 2013
50. Robertson, Ivan, and Cooper, Cary, *Well-Being, Productivity and Happiness at Work,* p. 3
51. Seligman, Martin, *Flourish,* p. 12
52. Seligman, Ibid, p. 17
53. Loehr, Jim and Schwartz, Tony *The Power of Full Engagement*
54. Csikszentmihalyi, Mihaly, *Activity and Happiness: towards a science of occupation,* Journal of Occupational Science, 1:1:1993
55. Sheldon, Kennon and Elliott, Andrew Journal of Personality and Social Psychology #76, 1999
56. Ben-Shahar, Tal, *Choose the Life you Want,* ch. 21
57. Nicolao, Leonardo et. al., *Happiness for Sale: do experiential purchases make consumers happier than material purchases?,* Journal of Consumer Research, August, 2009
58. Weil, Ibid, p.126
59. Berger, Bonnie G., Quest, National Association for Kinesiology in Higher Education, Volume 39, August, 1996
60. Blumenthal et. al., Archives of Internal Medicine, Vol.159
61. Mahncke et. al., Proceedings of the National Academy of Sciences, vol. 103, no. 33, 2006.
62. Dweck, Carol, *Mindset*
63. Kashdan, Todd and Steger, Michael, *Curiosity and pathways to well-being and meaning in life: Traits, states, and everyday behaviors,* Motivation and Emotion, September 2007
64. Lyubomirsky, Ibid, p.89
65. Emmons, Robert, *Thanks: How the New Science of Gratitude can Make you Happier,* Houghton Mifflin, 2007
66. Wood, Alex. et. al., *Gratitude predicts psychological well-being above the Big Five facets,* Personality and Individual Differences, Vol. 46, March, 2009

67. Lung Hung Chen & Ying Hwa Kee, Social Indicators Research, Vol. 89, Nov., 2008
68. Cohen, Ibid, p.15
69. Thoits, Peggy and Hewitt, Lyndi, *Volunteer Work and Wellbeing,* Journal of Health and Social Behavior, Vol. 42, 2001
70. Borgonovi, Francesca, *Doing Well by Doing Good,* Social Science and Medicine, June, 2008
71. New York Times, 12/28/13
72. Pressfield, Steven, *The War of Art*, p.39
73. Seligman, Ibid, p.20
74. Peterson, Park, and Seligman, *Orientations to happiness and life satisfaction: the full life versus the empty life*, Journal of Happiness Studies, Vol. 6, 2005

Acknowledgments

Thanks to all who helped directly or indirectly on this project. To the Positive Psychology community that finally made the study of human behavior useful to us ordinary people who want to create better lives for ourselves and those around us. Special thanks to Tal ben-Shahar, my teacher.

Thanks to readers and those with whom I bounced ideas along the way: Megan McDonough, Beulah Trey, Lynda Wallace, Shannon Kelly, Scott Simon, Fiona Trembath, Joe Kelley, Sheryl Sarnak, Hope Eaton, Kim Winnick, Jane Strunk Anderson, Diane Davies Visconti and Janet Sanders.

I am especially glad to be working with Jerry Dorris of AuthorSupport.com on book production.

Bibliography

Beck, Martha, *Finding Your Own North Star,* MJF Books, 2001

Ben-Shahar, Tal, *Happier,* McGraw Hill, 2007

Ben-Shahar, Tal, *Choose the Life you Want,* The Experiment Publishing, 2012

Bolton, Martha, *The Official Hugs Book,* Simon & Schuster, 2002

Cohen, Stuart, *The Seventh System: A Thinking Person's Guide to the Human Emotional System,* Mezuries, 2010

Csikszentmihalyi, Mihaly, *Flow,* Harper & Row, 1990

Dweck, Carol, *Mindset,* Ballantine Books, 2007

Fritz, Robert, *Creating,* Fawcett Columbine, 1991

Fritz, Robert, *The Path of Least Resistance,* Ballantine Books, 1989

Frederickson, Barbara, *Positivity,* Crown Publishers, 2009

Gibran, Khalil, *The Prophet,* Knopf, 1923

Gilbert, Daniel, *Stumbling on Happiness,* Vintage Books, 2007

Haidt, Jonathan, *The Happiness Hypothesis,* Basic Books, 2006

Kabat-Zinn, Jon, *Full Catastrophe Living: Using the Wisdom of Your Body and Mind to Face Stress, Pain and Illness,* Bantam, Revised edition 2013

Kahneman, Daniel, *Thinking Fast and Slow,* Farrar, Strauss and Giroux, 2011

Langer, Ellen, *Mindfulness,* Addison Wesley, 1989

Loehr, Jim and Schwartz, Tony, *The Power of Full Engagement,* Free Press, 2005

Lyubomrisky, Sonia, *The How of Happiness,* Penguin Press, 2007

Neff, Kristin, *Self Compassion: Stop Beating Yourself up and Leave Insecurity Behind*, Harper Collins, 2011

Pressfield, Steven, *The War of Art, Winning the Inner Creative Battle*, Rugged Land LLC, 2002

Ricard, Matthieu, *Happiness*, Hachette, 2003, translation 2006

Robertson, Ivan and Cooper, Cary, *Well-Being, Productivity and Happiness at Work*, Palgrave Macmillan, 2011

Rosenfeld, Alvin and Wise, Nicole, *Hyper-Parenting: Are You Hurting Your Child by Trying Too Hard*. Renamed *The Over-Scheduled Child*, St. Martin's Press, 2000

Ryan, Catherine Hyde, *Pay it Forward*, Simon & Schuster, 2014

Seligman, Martin, *Flourish*, Free Press, 2011

Stevens, Barry, *Don't Push the River It Flows by Itself*, Real People Press, 1970

Tolle, Eckhart, *The Power of Now*, Namaste Publishing, 2004

Weill, Andrew, *Spontaneous Happiness*, Little, Brown, 2011

Weiner, Eric, *The Geography of Bliss*, Hachette, 2008

www.ingramcontent.com/pod-product-compliance
Lightning Source LLC
Chambersburg PA
CBHW070615050426
42450CB00011B/3063